THE I-LOVE-AMERICA COLORING BOOK

HANNAH GOODING

ILLUSTRATED BY KIMMA PARISH

CASTLE POINT BOOKS

NEW YORK

LET FREEDOM RING.

Copyright © 2023 by St. Martin's Press.

All rights reserved. Printed in the United States of America.

For information, address St. Martin's Publishing Group,

120 Broadway, New York, NY 10271.

www.castlepointbooks.com

The Castle Point Books trademark is owned by Castle Point Publishing, LLC.

Castle Point books are published and distributed by St. Martin's Publishing Group.

ISBN 978-1-250-28727-4 (trade paperback)

Cover and interior art by Kimma Parish

Our books may be purchased in bulk for promotional, educational, or business use.

Please contact your local bookseller or the Macmillan Corporate and Premium Sales Department

at 1-800-221-7945, extension 5442, or by email at MacmillanSpecialMarkets@macmillan.com.

First Edition: 2023

10 9 8 7 6 5 4 3 2 1

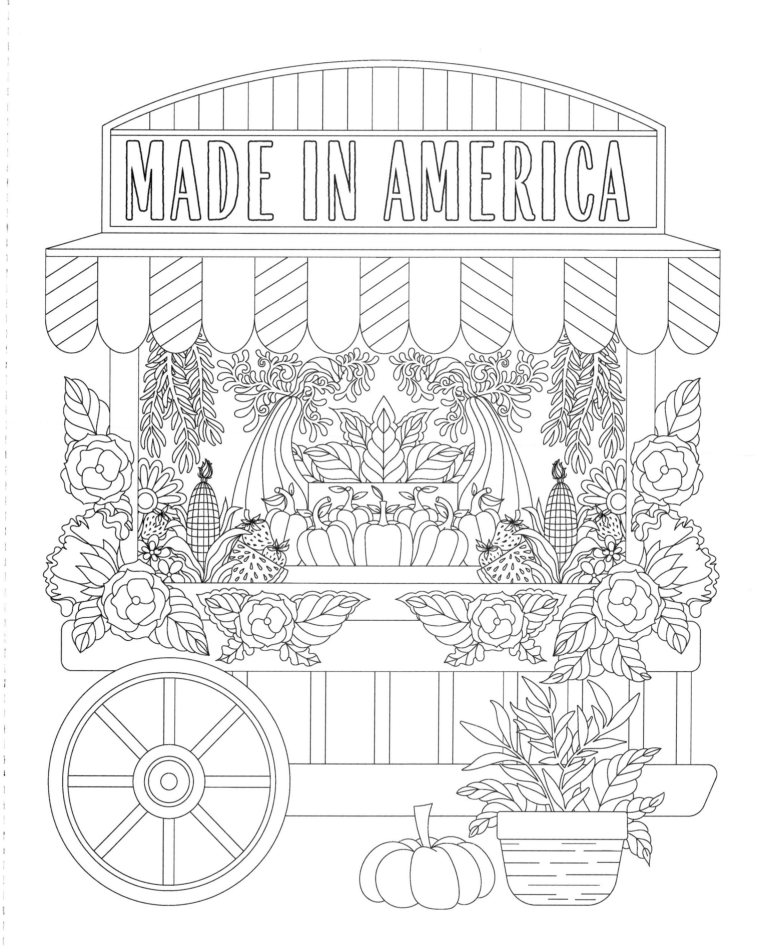